God's Covenant with You

The Bible Tells a Story

SCOTT HAHN

with Stratford Caldecott

Illustrated by David Clayton

Second Spring Catechesis

Published by

Second Spring

6a King Street, Oxford OX2 6DF, UK
www.secondspring.co.uk

Text © Scott Hahn and Stratford Caldecott.
Illustrations © David Clayton.
ALL RIGHTS RESERVED.

ISBN: 978-0-9555380-4-9

Printed in the UK by Joshua Horgan Print Partnership, Oxford.
UK orders to P.O. Box 2001, Petworth, GU28 9YA, UK (for US orders see website above).

CONTENTS

Introduction for Parents and Catechists 5

1. You were in the Garden with ADAM 7

2. You were in the Ark with NOAH. 11

3. You were homeless with ABRAHAM. 13

4. You were in the desert with MOSES 17

5. You saw the kingdom come with DAVID 21

6. You received new life with JESUS 25

7. You came out of the waters of BAPTISM 31

The Family of God: Three Angels of God with Abraham and Sarah (p. 13)

INTRODUCTION
For Parents and Catechists

I have written many books, but never one like this. In this Introduction I am speaking to parents and teachers, but in the book itself I am writing for children. We have kept the words as simple as possible, although the concepts behind them are profound. They are profound because they are God's concepts, not mine: they are the ideas he reveals to us in Scripture through the words and lives of the prophets.

Adults often talk down to children because they think children cannot grasp sophisticated notions. Sometimes that is true, but while their verbal abilities may be undeveloped, they are often more responsive than adults to natural symbolism, and they feel things more intensely. That is why a catechist or teacher needs to be sensitive to the impact of images and simple stories, as well as their importance in awakening a deep understanding. These simple stories drawn from Scripture can never be fully grasped; they always reveal more about God than we may be ready to hear and see.

Jesus himself used parables in his teaching, and these parables are inexhaustible. They can be read at many different levels, and the same is true of salvation history itself. In recent years we have become much more aware that God reveals himself in a story, a history, and that this history of the Jewish people also applies to each individual soul in its own journey to God. It is the history of a Covenant, or a series of Covenants – an ancient Covenant renewed over and over again, and extended to more and more people, until we are prepared for that most wonderful and most astounding of all Covenants: the new and everlasting one in Christ's Blood.

Those who are welcomed into this Covenant make up the Church, the New People of God, already present in figure in all the earlier Covenants. On our side the "story the Bible tells" is the story of a promise broken by us and renewed by God, broken and renewed, over and over again.… God is always faithful. In his love he never gives up. So, perhaps one of the most important lessons of this story is that we are loved with this kind of love.

The story the Bible tells, the story of the Covenant, is the story that, of all stories, we most need to hear, and to teach our children. It makes sense of our lives, and shows us why we are here. It shows us that we are loved. But too often, because the Bible is so big, we lose sight of this golden thread that runs all the way through it, and our children never learn what God wants them to know. That is why this book focuses on the theme of Covenant. This divine idea runs through the Bible, and it underlies all theology. If children begin to grasp it as a story that means something to them, a story in which they have a part, they will be well prepared for studying the Catechism when they are older.

In this book, David Clayton's beautiful pictures are just as important as the text. They offer a landscape for the child's imagination, in which the child may play freely, while listening to the words that accompany them. The pictures help bring the words to life, and a creative application of crayons to the pictures can help the story of the Covenant impress itself more deeply on the imagination. These pictures also bear intriguing traces of many artistic traditions, especially the wonderful iconography of the East and the illuminated manuscripts of the West. In this way a love of great Christian art may be enkindled here, alongside a love of Scripture.

God is beautiful and he loves beauty. May this book encourage teachers, parents and children to love beauty too, and to search for it until they find it in him.

Scott Hahn

For the doctrinal background to this book, see *The Catechism of the Catholic Church*, 51-73, 1267-70, 2562-4

See also:
Scott Hahn, *First Comes Love: Finding Your Family in the Church and the Trinity* (DLT and Doubleday, 2002)

Scott Hahn, *A Father Who Keeps His Promises: God's Covenant Love in Scripture* (Servant, 1998)

1
You were in the Garden with ADAM

God is a family – Father, Son, and Holy Spirit.

God made the first man (Adam), and with him the first woman (Eve). He breathed his own life into them, so they would be his children. He wanted them to be happy with him forever. He gave them a beautiful garden in a place called Eden.

The marriage of Adam and Eve was the very first Covenant. A "Covenant" is what happens when people give themselves to each other, making themselves into a family. Adam and Eve were a family with God.

Together Adam and Eve were supposed be God's family on earth, and to love one another the way God loves in heaven. Soon new life would come from this love, as they gave birth to their children.

God knew that Adam and his wife could only be happy with him forever if they loved him enough to do what he told them. So he told them they must never eat fruit from one of the trees in the garden, a very special tree called the Tree of the Knowledge of Good and Evil.

God knew that the Serpent who was in the garden would tempt them to eat from the Tree. By saying No to the Serpent they could say Yes to God. But when the Serpent came to them, he told Eve that the fruit would make them like God. He said that they would not die if they ate it. Adam should have protected his wife, but he was afraid. He could have said No to the Serpent. But he did not. Instead he joined Eve in eating the fruit.

Then Adam and Eve ran away, because they had turned their backs on God and taken the fruit instead. They had lost the divine life he had breathed into them and so they were afraid. At first they hid among the other trees in the garden. But God called them back to him. When they admitted what they had done, he told them what it really meant for them.

They would have to leave the garden, and later they would die because their bodies would turn back into the dust they were made from. He told them they had brought suffering into the world by what they had done. He also told them he still loved them and would continue to look after them in the hard life they must now lead.

Adam and his wife left the garden, and they could not come back because the way was guarded by a Holy Angel with a flaming sword. But because God was still determined to be faithful to his first Covenant and his children, to Adam and Eve and all their descendants, he promised he would watch over their family on earth, as it got bigger and bigger, and one day he would heal the damage they had caused.

One day Jesus would overcome the evil in the world, and he would even conquer death. But it would take a long time.

2
You were in the Ark with
NOAH

Outside the garden, Adam and Eve had many children and grandchildren before they died, and those in their turn had many more children, until there were lots of people on earth. Over time most of them became very wicked.

One day, only one man and his family in the whole world were still good. His name was Noah. So God decided to make his Covenant again with Noah. Through him and his family the first Covenant could still be fulfilled. It was not too late. There was still time for God's promises to come true.

So when all the world and its wickedness was swept away in a great Flood, God protected Noah and his family by telling him to build an Ark. This was a giant ship made of wood. Inside he could be safe from the waters, and there he could keep his family warm and dry, along with all the animals that could not swim, until the Flood went down.

After seven months the Flood did go down, and the Ark landed on a mountaintop. Then Noah with all his family, and all the animals that were in the Ark, went out into the muddy land, and when it was dry enough they made a garden.

Then God spoke to Noah, and made a new promise to him. He made a Covenant with him and with all the animals. The Covenant was sealed on an altar that Noah built on the dry land. And God sent a big rainbow to remind everyone of the Covenant, and to show that he would never destroy the world with water again.

Noah had three children: Shem, Ham, and Japheth. It is said that all the peoples of the earth alive today come from them. The peoples of Canaan, Babylon, and Egypt came from Ham, the tribes of Israel from Shem, and the others from Japheth. So Noah was like a new Adam, because all the children of the earth from now on would come from his family.

3
You were homeless with
ABRAHAM

A long time after Noah's death, one of his descendants was a man called Abram. He was living in a place called Haran with his wife Sarai. One day God spoke to him and told him to travel to a new land that he did not know. At the same time God made him three promises.

First, God said he would make Abram's descendants into a great nation. Abram and Sarai had no children yet, but God would give them many children, as many as the stars in the sky.

Second, God said he would make his name great. And third, God also said he would bless all the families of the earth through him. God then made these three promises into a Covenant. Abram believed God would do what he said, even though it was difficult for him to see how this would all happen.

Later, when Abram was 99 years old, God changed his name to Abraham, and his wife's name to Sarah. They still had no children of their own, and it was hard to believe that God could give them many children when they were so old. But Abraham knew God could do anything.

One day, as Abraham sat at the door of his tent looking out, resting in the hot sun, three men came out of the desert. These men were sent by God. They were really Angels, on their way to destroy the wicked cities of Sodom and Gomorrah. Abraham was not sure who they were, but he offered them a meal, and they stayed with him a while. While they were there, they told him that by next spring he and Sarah would have their first baby. Sarah laughed at this. She was so old that it seemed impossible. (Can you see Sarah laughing in the picture on the next page?)

Sure enough, by next spring the baby was born, and they called him Isaac.

When Isaac was old enough to walk and talk, God again did something very strange, to test Abraham. He told him to sacrifice his son – to kill him! Now Abraham knew that there is always a good reason for what God does, even if we can't see what it is straightaway, so he got ready to sacrifice his son. God did not really want Isaac to die, but he needed to know if Abraham would

trust him.

Just as God had promised, through Isaac many children were born to Abraham after all – as many as the stars in the sky! Isaac's son Jacob was called Israel, and was the father of the twelve Jewish tribes. And one of his grandsons was called Joseph, who rescued the Israelites during a great famine by taking them to live in Egypt, where he had become a friend of the king.

God never forgot his promises to Abraham.

4
You were in the desert with
MOSES

The first of God's promises to Abraham (to make his descendants into a great nation) came true through a man called Moses. This is how it happened.

At first it was good for the tribes of Israel in Egypt, but after Joseph died, they were made into slaves by the king of the Egyptians, called the Pharaoh. The Egyptians were afraid of the Israelites, there were so many of them, which is why they made them work so hard.

In the end, Pharaoh ordered all the new boy-children of the Israelites to be killed, but one of the boys was saved by his mother, who put him in a little basket of bulrushes and floated him on the River Nile. His sister hid and watched as a Princess, the daughter of the Pharaoh, found the basket and fell in love with the little baby, adopting him as her own son.

She called him Moses. He grew up as a prince in Egypt, but when he was older he became angry with the way the Israelites were treated, and ran away into the desert. There he joined some wandering tribes, fell in love, and got married. But God had much bigger plans for Moses.

One day, God appeared to him in the form of a burning bush, calling him by his name out of the fire. The voice said that the God of Abraham, Isaac and Joseph had an important task for him to do. Moses must go back to Pharaoh and ask permission to bring all his people away into the desert with him, to worship God there.

When Moses went back to Egypt, Pharaoh refused to do as God asked, even though Moses performed miracles to prove he was sent by God. Instead he made the Israelites work even harder.

In order to persuade Pharaoh to let them go, God sent a series of disasters to Egypt – ten plagues, ending with the death of all the eldest sons of the Egyptians, including Pharaoh's own son. The Israelites were told by Moses to eat a Passover meal that night, and the Angel of Death passed over their houses, leaving their sons alive.

Now that his own son was dead, Pharaoh let them go, but soon he changed his mind and chased them as far as the Red Sea, where God's Angel had led them. God moved the waters aside for Israel to pass through safely, but when the Egyptian army followed, they were drowned in the sea.

Three months later, the twelve tribes arrived at Mount Sinai. There Moses went up the mountain and received the Ten Commandments to give them. This Law was going to be the new sign of their Covenant with God. God had told them he would make them a great nation, a nation of priests to show all other nations how to be holy, and now he wanted to fulfil that promise.

In order to talk with God, Moses disappeared into the fiery cloud on top of Mount Sinai for forty days. During that time, the tribes got bored and changed their minds, even after promising God to be faithful to him, and they started worshipping a Golden Calf instead. When Moses came back he told them how angry God was. They would have to wander for forty more years through the desert before they came to Canaan, the Promised Land.

Moses had made his people into a great nation, with a great Law to bind them together under God. In the end, when they came to Canaan, they had a home of their own at last.

Jesus, too, would escape being killed as a child by being taken into Egypt, and he too led his people to freedom and made them holy, though in a different way from Moses. He too spoke with God face to face, and he too offered his own life for the sake of his people. In God's great plan, Moses was a step on the way to Jesus, who was not a prophet but the Son of God.

On the next page you will see a picture of Moses and the Burning Bush.

5
You saw the kingdom coming with
DAVID

All through history, and in our lives, it is the same story. God tries to make us holy again, so that we will be able to live with him in heaven. We like the idea at first, but then we get bored, or change our minds, or forget. Then God has to find a way to bring us back to him. Sometimes it is only when something really bad happens that we remember what we promised to God. But God is always faithful to us, and always does what he promises, even if it takes a long time.

God's second promise to Abraham was fulfilled through David. (Do you remember what the first promise was?) His second promise was to make his name great, and so now he made Abraham's descendant David into a very great king.

After Moses, the people of Israel had been ruled by Judges, until they asked God for a king to rule them. Then the prophet Samuel anointed as king a man called Saul, but Saul did not always do what God commanded. So God chose a young shepherd boy called David,

21

the son of Jesse, to be the second king of his People.

David was very good looking, and he could sing and play the harp as well as look after sheep. But no one had ever expected him to become king of Israel! Apart from anything else, he had seven brothers who were older and stronger than him. But God always knows what he is doing.

David showed he was a good warrior even as a boy, when he killed a giant called Goliath using only a slingshot. Later when he was king, he established the royal city in Jerusalem, which became known as David's City. This was the same place where Abraham had long ago offered Isaac to God, and where he had received God's blessing.

David loved God very much, and he wrote many of the Psalms, which are the prayers and songs of Israel that you will find in the heart of the Bible. He was like a priest as well as a king, and he wanted to build a great Temple to God in Jerusalem, where the Ark of the Covenant could be kept. (This contained the Ten Commandments and it was the most holy thing in Israel.) The Temple would be the new sign of God's everlasting Covenant, his presence with his People.

In the end, God did not let David build his Temple, because David was nearly always at war. Instead, he let the Temple be built by David's son, King Solomon the Magnificent. That Temple became one of the wonders of the world.

But God had made Abraham's name great through David, and now he made a promise to David that his kingdom would fill the whole world. The kingdom would be much bigger than Israel: it would be the Kingdom of God. Its ruler would be one of the children who descended from David: Jesus of Nazareth.

David and his son Solomon were like "pictures" of what Jesus would be – the great King of all the earth, full of beauty and wisdom. The Temple, too, was a sign of Jesus, who would make the Covenant with all men in his own blood. But Jesus would come in a way that people did not expect, and his glory would look very different from that of David and Solomon.

6
You received new life with
JESUS

The sons of David were sometimes wise and good, but more often they were wicked. None of them was really worthy of God's great promise to David, until one day, many years later….

In Jesus all the promises of God came true, including the third promise to Abraham, when God said he would bless all the families of the earth through his children.

Jesus was the son of the Virgin Mary, and although God was his Father, he was also in the family of Joseph, a carpenter who descended from King David and from Abraham. Jesus was human, but he was also the Son of God, and he came to make a new Covenant with all of us.

Joseph's family was very poor, and at times they were homeless, like Abraham and Moses. When Jesus was born, God's Angels went to tell the shepherds to come and see him – shepherds like the one David had been as a boy. A bad king, called Herod, tried to kill Jesus, but Joseph took him into Egypt to keep him safe until the danger was past.

When he grew up he was baptized by his cousin John in the river Jordan, and the Holy Spirit showed himself to him, and his Father spoke to him from heaven.

After that, Jesus knew it was time to teach everyone who would listen that God's Kingdom was coming, and he performed many miracles. But he told them that this Kingdom was not like any of the kingdoms they already knew: it would be much better. It would be a kingdom of love. But many people did not like the idea of a kingdom of love. They wanted a kingdom like the ones they knew.

Jesus made the new Covenant with his disciples. Together they sat down to eat a Passover meal according to the Law of Moses. But Jesus turned the Passover meal into the Sacrament of his new Covenant. This time the Passover would be to remember not just the escape of Moses and the Jews from Egypt, but everyone's escape from death and sin through Jesus Christ. It was called the Last Supper. It was called "Last" because it was the last one that Jesus ate before he was crucified.

All of us have to die because of sin – beginning with Adam and Eve. Jesus knew that his enemies wanted to kill him for saying he was the Son of God, and for teaching about the new Kingdom. So he was going to let himself be killed in our place, as if he too had sinned and deserved to die. Then he would rise from the dead so that we could live for ever too.

The Last Supper began as he sat down with his disciples, and it ended on the Cross when he was crucified the next day. It ended when the soldiers gave him sour wine to drink from a sponge.

This was going to be a Covenant in which all human beings could share. So at every Mass, the priest repeats the words of Jesus, and the bread and wine offered by the priest become the Body and Blood of Jesus. In that way the Mass makes us part of the Last Supper and the Covenant Jesus made on the Cross.

After Jesus was killed and laid in the Tomb, he came back to life, to live for ever. If we become part of his body through the Covenant, we will also come back to life after we die, and live for ever with him in the kingdom of love. But how do we become part of his body? The next chapter will show you.

In his covenants with Adam, Noah, Abraham, Moses, and David, God opened membership in his family to ever more people: first to a married couple, then to a household, then to a tribe, then to a nation, then to a kingdom - till, finally, the invitation was made to all of us in Jesus. Christ's family consists of all who receive new birth as children of God through baptism (John 3:3-8), and who continue to share his life through the sacraments. We become his younger brothers and sisters.

*"What no eye has seen, nor ear heard,
Nor the heart of man conceived,
What God has prepared for those who love him",
God has revealed to us through the Spirit.*
(Cor. 2: 9-10)

7
You came out of the waters of
BAPTISM

How did you become part of the body of Christ? You may not remember when you were baptized, but when that happened, that was when you began to belong to Jesus and his family. You followed Jesus into the waters where he was baptized, and the Holy Spirit came to be with you, and inside you, to help you to pray, and to hear the Father's voice.

The other Sacraments will help you to follow Jesus all the way to the Cross. When you say sorry for your sins in Confession and when you receive Jesus in Holy Communion, you are becoming one of his disciples at the Last Supper, when he gave himself to them.

Jesus says, "Listen! I am standing and knocking at your door. If you hear my voice and open the door, I will come in and we will eat together."

You are part of his family, the family that he makes through his sacrifice. By giving himself up for you, he makes you part of his new family. So what joins you to Jesus is his love for you, and your love for him. And if you love him you will try to do what he wants you to do.

Mary is your mother, in God's family. As God's child, you have a family all around the world, on earth and in heaven. The Catholic Church is God's worldwide family that the Father sent the Son to establish by the Spirit. The Angels and all the Saints who have gone before you are your older brothers and sisters.

If you walk with Jesus, one day he will lead you to your true home in heaven, where everyone loves you, and where you will learn your secret name, the one that only you and God can know. That will be the beginning of an adventure that goes on forever.